Served from the Swedish Kitchen

FIFTY CLASSIC RECIPES FROM SWEDEN

ICA BOKFÖRLAG

The Swedish Kitchen

Welcome on a culinary journey through Sweden.

The opportunity to experience a country with all five senses, but especially with those of smell and taste.

From north to south, from forest to open fields, from the heart of the country to the seashore. The whole spectrum of flavors, from savory to sweet, boiled to fried, hot to cold.

Is there any better way to experience a country than through its flavors?

Sweden is a long, sparsely populated country, which stretches far to the north, past the Arctic Circle. A country with rich vegetation and four distinct seasons, thanks to warm air currents.

Nowhere in the world are the four seasons – icy winter, blossoming spring, blooming summer and fiery autumn – so defined as in Sweden.

All this has influenced the Swedish kitchen. Swedish food is world-famous because it covers such a wide range.

In this book, we have chosen some of the most classic dishes from the Swedish kitchen. Chef Malin Söderström, former member of the Swedish national culinary team, feels that food is an important part of our cultural heritage, and she has carefully updated the Swedish traditional kitchen for us. Her dishes are based on recipes that have been favorites for more than 100 years, and we hope they will still be enjoyed 100 years from now.

Have a little taste of Sweden! We hope you will be back for more.

Note: When preparing these recipes, use either deciliters or cups (in parentheses). Do not combine the two methods of measurement in the same recipe.

THE ROYAL PALACE, STOCKHOLM

Stuffed cabbage rolls

Kåldolmar

4 SERVINGS

1/2 DL (3 1/2 TABLESPOONS) LONG-GRAIN
RICE
I MEDIUM HEAD CABBAGE
I SMALL ONION, CHOPPED
I TABLESPOON BUTTER
150 G (5 OZ) GROUND BEEF
150 G (6 OZ) GROUND PORK
I 1/2 DL (SCANT 2/3 CUP) MILK
SALT AND PEPPER
1/2 TABLESPOON DARK CORN SYRUP

Cook rice according to package
directions.

Core cabbage and separate leaves slightly.
Place cabbage, core side up, in a pot of
boiling, salted water. Remove leaves as
they soften and drain on a kitchen
towel. Cut out coarse central veins.

Fry onion in 1 teaspoon of the butter
until shiny. Combine with rice and
ground meat. Gradually add milk, then
season with salt and pepper. The mixture
will be loose. Place a tablespoon of meat
mixture on each cabbage leaf. Fold sides
over meat, then roll up.

Brown remaining butter in a skillet.
Fry several cabbage rolls at a time.
Do not crowd. Drizzle syrup over
cabbage rolls and fry until golden.
Transfer to a pot, deglaze pan with
cooking juices and pour over cabbage
rolls. Simmer slowly over low heat until
cabbage is soft, about 30 minutes.

Transfer cabbage rolls to a serving
platter. Thicken cooking liquid if
desired, or reduce by half over high
heat. Serve with sauce, boiled potatoes
and lingonberry compote.

This is a Swedish version of Turkish stuffed
grape leaves. King Karl XII brought the recipe
to Sweden more than 300 years ago. He
substituted cabbage for grape leaves.

Pea soup with salt pork

Ärter med rimmat fläsk

4 SERVINGS

5 DL (2 CUPS) DRIED YELLOW PEAS
(WHOLE)
2 LITERS (8 CUPS) WATER
400–500 G (1 LB) SALT PORK,
SHOULDER OR FLANK, IN ONE PIECE
2 CLOVES
1 ONION, PEELED
2 TEASPOONS THYME
2 TEASPOONS MARJORAM
2 KNOCKWURSTS (8–9 OZ)

Rinse peas and soak in water overnight.
Drain, then add water and bring to a
boil. Skim well, removing as many hulls
as possible. Stir with a balloon whisk,
which traps hulls easily.

While peas are simmering, add pork.
Stick cloves into onion and add with
thyme and marjoram. Make sure peas
do not burn.

After a couple of hours, both peas and
pork should be cooked. Remove pork
and slice. Season soup to taste and
serve in deep bowls with pork alongside.
Serve with hearty mustard.

Some people like sausage in their soup.
If using knockwursts, prick well, so they
won't burst. Add toward end of cooking
time. Slice and serve with pork. This
dish also can be made with split peas.
It takes less time, because split peas do
not require soaking, and they cook in
less than half the time. Split pea soup
will not be so hearty and flavorful as
this time-honored method.

Pea soup is served throughout Sweden
every Thursday, often with thin pancakes
for dessert. This has been a tradition
since the Middle Ages, when a hearty
meal was served the evening before
a fast day, which was every Friday at
that time.

Fried Baltic herring with mashed potatoes

Stekta strömmingsflundror med potatismos

4 SERVINGS

600 G (1 1/3 LB) BALTIC HERRING
FILLETS (ANY SMALL OILY FISH CAN
BE SUBSTITUTED)
1/2 DL (3 1/2 TABLESPOONS) FINELY
CHOPPED FRESH DILL (DO NOT USE
DRIED DILL)
50 G (3 TABLESPOONS) BUTTER
SALT AND FRESHLY GROUND WHITE PEPPER
1 DL (1/2 CUP) ALL-PURPOSE FLOUR
2–3 EGGS, LIGHTLY BEATEN
1 DL (1/2 CUP) FINE BREADCRUMBS
BUTTER

Clean and rinse fish. Dry well. Remove
fins.

Beat dill into butter, then add salt and
pepper to taste. Arrange half the fillets
skin side down. Spread with dill butter.
Top with remaining fillets, skin side up.

Season flour with salt. Dip double fillets
in flour, then in beaten egg, then in
crumbs. Press crumbs onto fillets so
they stay on. Fry in a generous amount
of butter over high heat.

Serve piping hot with mashed potatoes.

Leftover fried herring are delicious when
marinated in a brine made of one part
vinegar, two parts sugar, three parts
water, bay leaf, sliced onion and allspice.

Mashed potatoes
4 SERVINGS

1 KG (2 1/2 LB) POTATOES (DO NOT
USE NEW POTATOES)
2 TEASPOONS SALT PER LITER (QUART)
WATER
2–2 1/2 DL (1 CUP) MILK
40 G (2 1/2 TABLESPOONS) BUTTER
FRESHLY GROUND WHITE PEPPER

Peel potatoes and cut into chunks. Boil
in salted water, drain and steam until all
moisture has evaporated. Press through
a ricer or mash.

Heat milk and add gradually. Beat in
butter until light and fluffy. Season with
salt and freshly ground white pepper.

Sailor's steak

Sjömansbiff

4 SERVINGS

600 G (1 1/3 LB) BONELESS ROUND STEAK,
IN 8 SLICES
600 G (1 1/3 LB) MEDIUM POTATOES
2 MEDIUM ONIONS
2 TABLESPOONS BUTTER
2 TEASPOONS SALT
WHITE PEPPER
3–5 DL (1 1/4–2 CUPS) WATER OR
BOUILLON MIXED WITH BEER,
OR JUST BEER
1 BAY LEAF
1 TWIG THYME
CHOPPED PARSLEY

Trim meat of any fat and membrane.
Pound lightly to flatten.

Peel and cut potatoes into thick slices.
Peel and cut onion into thin slices. In
a large skillet with a lid, brown onion
in a small amount of the butter. Set
aside. Brown meat on both sides and
season with salt and white pepper. Add
liquid and herbs. Cover and simmer
about 10 minutes.

Preheat oven to 125°C (250°F). Layer
potato slices, meat, and onion in an
ovenproof dish, beginning and ending
with potatoes. Add liquid to level of top
layer. Cover with buttered parchment
paper, then cover with lid and bake
1–1 1/2 hours, until meat is tender.
This dish also can be prepared on top
of the stove.

Sprinkle with parsley and serve
immediately.

Egg-anchovy salad

Gubbröra

4 SERVINGS

4–5 HARD-COOKED EGGS
1 TIN SWEDISH-STYLE ANCHOVIES
(100 G, 3 1/2 OZ)
1 SMALL RED ONION
3–4 TABLESPOONS FINELY CHOPPED
FRESH DILL (DO NOT USE DRIED DILL)
1 TABLESPOON SWEDISH CAVIAR
(FROM A TUBE)

Peel and coarsely chop eggs. Cube
anchovies and mince onion. Combine
all ingredients and serve cold. This
mixture is good on crispbread.

NB There is no real substitute for
Swedish caviar, but golden caviar
also makes a delicious salad.

Jansson's temptation

Janssons frestelse

4–6 SERVINGS

1 KG (2 1/4 LB) POTATOES (DO NOT
USE NEW POTATOES)
2 ONIONS
BUTTER
100 G (3 1/2 OZ) SWEDISH-STYLE
ANCHOVY FILLETS AND BRINE
4 DL (1 2/3 CUPS) WHIPPING CREAM
2 TABLESPOONS BREADCRUMBS

Preheat oven to 250°C (425°F). Peel and
cut potatoes into strips. Do not rinse
potatoes, as their starch thickens the
sauce. Peel onions and cut into thin
slices. Sauté in 1 tablespoon butter until
soft. Generously grease a deep, straight-
sided ovenproof dish. Layer potatoes,
onion, and anchovies, ending with
potatoes.

Press down lightly to even out surface,
Pour over cream almost to top of
potatoes. Sprinkle with anchovy brine.
Sprinkle with breadcrumbs and dot with
butter. Bake about 45 minutes.

Kalops with pickled beets

Kalops med inlagda rödbetor

4 SERVINGS

800 G (1 3/4 LB) LEAN BEEF STEW MEAT,
IN LARGE CUBES
4 ONIONS
1 LARGE CARROT
BUTTER
SALT AND FRESHLY GROUND WHITE PEPPER
ALL-PURPOSE FLOUR
3/4 DL (1/3 CUP) WATER
2 BAY LEAVES
10 ALLSPICE BERRIES
2 ANCHOVY FILLETS, MINCED OR 3–4
TABLESPOONS ANCHOVY BRINE, IF DESIRED

Trim meats of any fat and membrane.
Peel onions and cut into wedges. Scrape
and slice carrot. Brown butter in a large
pot, then brown meat, onion and carrot.
Season with salt and pepper, sprinkle
with flour, then add water, bay leaves
and allspice. Cover and simmer about
one hour, until meat is tender. Season
with salt, pepper, and anchovy.

Serve kalops directly from the cooking
pot with boiled potatoes and pickled
beets.

Pickled beets
1 KG (2 1/4 LB) SMALL, WHOLE FRESH
BEETS
3 3/4 DL (1 2/3 CUPS) 7% VINEGAR
2 3/4 DL (1 1/8 CUPS) WATER
1/2 DL (3 1/2 TABLESPOONS) SUGAR
6–7 WHOLE CLOVES

Brush beets well, but do not peel or cut
off tip of root. Simmer in lightly salted
water until tender. It takes much longer
in winter than in summer, when beets
are young and fresh. Let cool in cooking
water, then peel.

Combine remaining ingredients and
bring to a boil. Slice beets, then add
to brine. Marinate at least 24 hours
before serving.

Mashed root vegetables

Rotmos

4 SERVINGS

1 RUTABAGA (ABOUT 300 G, 10 OZ)
300 G (10 OZ) POTATOES
200 G (7 OZ) CARROTS
BUTTER
SALT AND FRESHLY GROUND WHITE PEPPER
PINCH GROUND ALLSPICE (IF DESIRED)

Clean, peel and cube rutabaga. Simmer
in salted water just to cover about 30
minutes. Peel and cube potatoes and
carrots and add. Simmer until tender.
There should not be much liquid
remaining.

Press through a ricer or mash with
cooking liquid, butter, salt, freshly
ground white pepper and a pinch of
allspice, if desired. Serve piping hot
with ham, corned beef or smoked lamb
dishes and good quality mustard.

Pressed cucumbers

Pressgurka

6 SERVINGS

1 SNAKE CUCUMBER
1/4 TEASPOON SALT
1 DL (1/3 CUP) 7% VINEGAR
1/2 DL (3 1/2 TABLESPOONS) SUGAR
1/4 TEASPOON WHITE PEPPER
2 TABLESPOONS FINELY CHOPPED PARSLEY

Peel and thinly slice cucumber
(preferably with a cheese plane).
Place in a bowl, cover with plastic
wrap, then weight down with a couple
of cans for 10 minutes. Pour off released
liquid and combine with vinegar,
sugar and pepper, stirring until sugar
has dissolved. Pour over cucumbers
and sprinkle with parsley.

Uppsala stew

Uppsalastuvning

4 SERVINGS

600 G (1 1/3 LB) CORNED BEEF BRISKET
2 BAY LEAVES
1 TWIG FRESH THYME
8 WHITE PEPPERCORNS
6 ALLSPICE BERRIES
2 ONIONS
500 G (1 LB) POTATOES
400 G (14 OZ) CARROTS
200 G (7 OZ) CELERIAC
200 G (7 OZ) RUTABAGA
CHOPPED PARSLEY

Proportions:
1/3 MEAT
2/3 VEGETABLES

Rinse meat in cold water and place in
a pot. (It should be a snug fit.) Add cold
water to barely cover. Bring to a boil,
skimming well. Add bay leaves, thyme,
pepper and allspice. Cover and simmer
about 1 1/2 hours. If meat pulls apart
easily with a fork, it is done. Remove
from cooking liquid and weigh down.

Peel vegetables and cut into chunks.
Add to cooking liquid and simmer until
tender. Slice meat and heat with
vegetables in bouillon.

Sprinkle with chopped parsley and
serve.

Uppsala and Lund are centers of education
and learning in Sweden. Uppsala stew has a lot
of class.

14

REINDEER, LAPPLAND

Reindeer Stroganoff

Renskavspanna

4 SERVINGS

3 DL (1 1/4 CUPS) CHANTERELLES
2 ONIONS, MINCED
5 JUNIPER BERRIES, CRUSHED
BUTTER
4 DL (1 2/3 CUPS) WHIPPING CREAM
450 G (1 LB) FROZEN REINDEER
TOP ROUND
SALT AND FRESHLY GROUND
WHITE PEPPER
2 TABLESPOONS CHOPPED PARSLEY

Brown chanterelles, onion and juniper
berries in butter. Add cream and reduce
by half, until thickened.

Thinly slice reindeer. Brown in butter
in a hot skillet. Pour over sauce and
simmer a few minutes. Season with
salt and pepper. Sprinkle with parsley.

Serve with mashed potatoes and
lingonberry compote.

In Sweden, reindeer are not associated with
Christmas. They are an important source of
income for the Sami, the indigenous people
of northern Sweden. Of all recipes for reindeer
meat, this one is the most popular.

Racks of deer with almond potato puree and mushrooms

Hjortracks med svamp
och mandelpotatispuré

4 SERVINGS

800 G (1 3/4 LB) RACKS OF DEER (ON
THE BONE)
50 G (3 TABLESPOONS) BUTTER
SALT AND PEPPER
600 G (1 1/3 LB) ALMOND POTATOES,
PEELED
2 DL (3/4 CUP) HALF AND HALF
25 G (1 1/2 TABLESPOONS) BUTTER
200 G (7–8 OZ) MIXED WILD MUSHROOMS
1 SHALLOT, MINCED
2 DL (3/4 CUP) RED WINE SAUCE
(SEE RECIPE AT RIGHT)

Preheat oven to 125°C (260°F). Brown
meat in butter, sprinkle with salt and
pepper. Roast until meat reaches an
internal temperature of 60°C (140°F),
about 1 hour.

Boil potatoes in salted water. Press
through a ricer, then beat in half and
half, butter, salt and pepper.

Sauté mushrooms lightly, then add shallot
and cook until soft.

Bring sauce to a boil. Pour over mushrooms and bring to a boil.

When meat is ready, remove from
oven, wrap in aluminum foil and let
rest 15 minutes.

Cut meat between ribs. Salt and pepper
cut surfaces. Place a mound of potatoes
on each plate with a large, wet spoon.
Spoon some mushrooms alongside.
Arrange meat on mushrooms (resting on
potatoes) and drizzle sauce all around

Red wine sauce
4 SERVINGS

2 SHALLOTS
1 SMALL CARROT
25 G (1 1/2 TABLESPOONS) BUTTER
1 TABLESPOON TOMATO PASTE
1 BOTTLE (3 CUPS) RED WINE
5 DL (2 CUPS) VEAL STOCK
1 TEASPOON ROSEMARY
SALT AND PEPPER
1 TABLESPOON CORNSTARCH STIRRED
INTO 1 TABLESPOON COLD WATER
(IF NEEDED)
1 TABLESPOON BUTTER

Peel and slice shallots and carrot.
Brown in butter until golden. Add
tomato paste and cook until dry. Add
a splash of wine and scrape pan with
a wooden spatula. When most of the
wine has evaporated, add a little more,
continuing until half the bottle (1 1/2
cups) is used up. Add remaining wine,
stock and rosemary. Simmer until 4 dl
(1 2/3 cups) remain. Strain and season
with salt and pepper. If sauce is too
thin, add cornstarch mixture and boil
until thickened. Just before serving,
beat in butter.

Meatballs (Cover picture)

Köttbullar

4 SERVINGS

1 DL (1/2 CUP) FRESH BREAD CRUMBS
2 DL (1 CUP) MILK
1 ONION, MINCED
BUTTER
300 G (10 OZ) GROUND BEEF
100 G (4 OZ) GROUND PORK
1 EGG
SALT, WHITE PEPPER, ALLSPICE
(IF DESIRED)

Sauce:
2 TABLESPOONS BUTTER
2 TABLESPOONS ALL-PURPOSE FLOUR
3 DL (1 1/4 CUPS) BEEF STOCK (OR
BOUILLON FROM A CUBE)
1 DL (1/2 CUP) BEER
2 TABLESPOONS LINGONBERRIES
SALT AND PEPPER

Soak breadcrumbs in milk. Brown onion
in butter.

Combine ground meat, bread mixture,
onion, and egg. Season with salt and
pepper – a little ground allspice is
especially nice around Christmas. Mix
lightly, adding a little water, if needed.

Do not overmix, as mixture is sensitive
to heat. Make a trial meatball, fry and
check for seasoning. Make small balls
with a wet hand and a spoon. It is a
good idea to have two spoons in a glass
of hot water and alternate between
meatballs. Place meatballs on a rinsed
plate.

The center of Swedish gastronomy, the heart
of the Swedish kitchen, the reigning master
of the Swedish table. That's the meatball.
"Swedish Meatballs" are world-famous. This
dish has been made immortal by not only our
own star chefs, but even by the Swedish chef
on "The Muppet Show". In the contemporary
Swedish kitchen, meatballs still have their
honored place on the Christmas table, but
they are also a favorite everyday dish
throughout the year, especially with children.
They are usually served with spaghetti
or mashed potatoes.

Fry meatballs in butter. Do not fry too
many at once. Shake pan frequently, so
they stay round. Place cooked meatballs
in an ovenproof dish or pot.

For sauce, brown butter in a saucepan,
then whisk in flour. Whisk in stock
and beer. Bring to a boil and simmer
10 minutes, until flour flavor has
disappeared. Stir in lingonberries and
season with salt and pepper.

Serve with mashed potatoes,
lingonberry compote and pickles.

Christmas ham

Julskinka

3 KG (6 1/2 LB) BONELESS HAM

Preheat oven to 150°C (300°F). Rinse
ham lightly in cold water. Wrap in
aluminum foil. Insert meat thermometer
into thickest part. Place on a rack
over an oven pan. Bake until internal
temperature reaches 70°C (158°F).
Count on 1–1 1/2 hours cooking time
per kilo (2 1/4 lb) ham. Remove from
oven and remove rind.

Mustard-crumb topping:
1 EGG
3 TABLESPOONS PREPARED MUSTARD
(DO NOT USE HOT DOG MUSTARD)
1 TEASPOON SUGAR
2–3 TABLESPOONS DRY, FINE
BREADCRUMBS

Preheat oven to 200°F (400°C).
Place ham on a rack over an oven
pan. Combine egg, mustard and sugar.
Brush or spread over ham. Sift over
breadcrumbs. Bake until golden.

Serve Christmas ham with mustard,
applesauce and pickled red cabbage.

Christmas bread

Jullimpa

1 BREAD

6 DL (2 1/2 CUPS) CULTURED BUTTERMILK
3 DL (1 1/4 CUPS) GOLDEN SYRUP OR
DARK CORN SYRUP
4 TEASPOONS BAKING SODA
7 DL (3 CUPS) SIFTED RYE FLOUR
2 DL (3/4 CUP) ALL-PURPOSE FLOUR
1 DL (1/2 CUP) RAISINS

Preheat oven to 175°C (350°F). Grease
and flour a 2 1/2 liter (10 cup) loaf pan.

Combine buttermilk and syrup in
a large bowl. Combine dry ingredients,
then sift over buttermilk mixture.
Mix lightly, then stir in raisins. Pour
into pan.

Bake about 75 minutes. Cover with
aluminum foil if bread becomes too
dark. Cool 10 minutes before removing
from pan.

Beef roulades

Oxrulader

4 SERVINGS

600 G (1 1/3 LB) BONELESS TOP ROUND OF
BEEF, IN 4 OR 8 THIN SLICES
1/2 TEASPOON SALT
1/4 TEASPOON GROUND BLACK PEPPER
3–4 TABLESPOONS CHOPPED ONION
BUTTER
2 TABLESPOONS LIGHT DIJON MUSTARD
2 PICKLES
5 DL (2 CUPS) VEAL STOCK
1–2 TABLESPOONS ALL-PURPOSE FLOUR
1 DL (1/2 CUP) WHIPPING CREAM

Spread out meat slices. Sprinkle lightly
with salt and pepper. Sauté onion in
butter and combine with mustard.

Slice pickles. Arrange a strip of onion
and pickle along one short side of each
slice of meat. Roll up and secure with
a wooden pick.

Heat butter in a heavy skillet with a lid.
Brown roulades on all sides. Add stock,
cover and simmer slowly until tender,
about 1 hour. Remove and set aside.
Strain cooking juices. Place flour
and cream in a lidded jar and shake.
Add to cooking juices. Simmer a few
minutes, until thickened. Correct
seasoning. Return roulades to pan
and heat through.

Serve with boiled potatoes and
lingonberry compote.

Braised steak

Slottsstek

8 SERVINGS

1 1/2 KG (3 1/4 LB) BONELESS BEEF
ROUND STEAK, IN ONE PIECE
2 TABLESPOONS BUTTER
2–3 RED ONIONS
1–1 1/2 TEASPOONS SALT
12 WHITE OR BLACK PEPPERCORNS
1 BAY LEAF
1 TABLESPOON VINEGAR
2–3 TABLESPOONS DARK CORN SYRUP
6–8 SWEDISH-STYLE ANCHOVY FILLETS
5 DL (2 CUPS) BEEF STOCK (OR
BOUILLON) OR WATER

Sauce:
4 DL (1 2/3 CUPS) COOKING LIQUID
2–3 TABLESPOONS ALL-PURPOSE FLOUR
STIRRED INTO 2 TABLESPOONS COLD
WATER
1–2 DL (1/2–3/4 CUP) WHIPPING CREAM
1/2–1 TEASPOON WORCESTERSHIRE SAUCE

Trim meat, removing all fat and
membrane. Dry with paper towels.
Brown meat slowly in butter over
medium heat. Insert meat thermometer
into thickest part.

Peel and slice onion and add. Salt meat
and add pepper, bay leaf, vinegar, syrup
and anchovies.

Lower heat and add stock or water.
Cover and braised until internal
temperature reaches 70°C (160°F),
about 1 1/2–2 hours.

Remove meat, wrap in aluminum foil
and let rest about 15 minutes.

Strain and measure cooking liquid.
If too much, reduce to desired amount.
If too little, add water or stock. Whisk
in flour-water mixture and simmer 2–3
minutes, until thickened. Make sure
that it does not burn.

Lower heat. Whisk in cream and
Worcestershire sauce. Correct
seasoning, if necessary.

Cut meat into thin, even slices.
Arrange on a serving platter. Serve
with vegetables, such as peas or beans,
boiled potatoes and sauce.

Lamb in dill

Dillkött

4 SERVINGS

1 KG (2 1/4 LB) BONELESS LAMB FLANK
OR BRISKET

Per liter water:
3/4 TABLESPOON SALT
3–4 WHITE PEPPERCORNS
1 LEEK, SLICED
1 SMALL CARROT, SLICED
CHOPPED DILL STALKS

Dill sauce:
1 TABLESPOON BUTTER
2 TABLESPOONS ALL-PURPOSE FLOUR
4 DL (1 2/3 CUPS) COOKING LIQUID
2 1/2 TEASPOONS SUGAR
1–1 1/2 TABLESPOONS VINEGAR
1/2 DL (3 1/2 TABLESPOONS) FINELY
CHOPPED DILL
1 EGG YOLK
1/2 DL (3 1/2 TABLESPOONS) WHIPPING
CREAM

Cut meat into fairly large serving pieces.
Place in salted water and bring to a boil.
Remove from heat and rinse immediately
in cold running water.

Place meat in a large pot and add water
to barely cover. Bring to a boil. Skim
well, then add salt, peppercorns, leek,
carrot and dill. Simmer over low heat
until meat is tender (1–1 1/2 hours).
Transfer to a serving casserole and
keep warm.

Melt butter in a heavy saucepan. Whisk
in flour, then add 2 dl (3/4 cup) of the
cooking liquid, whisking constantly.
Add remaining 2 dl (3/4 cup) cooking
liquid and simmer until slightly reduced.
Dissolve sugar in vinegar, then add
enough to sauce to give it a sweet-sour
flavor. Stir in dill. Whisk egg yolk into
cream and whisk into sauce. Do not
allow sauce to boil after dill and egg
yolk are added.

Pour sauce over meat and serve with
boiled potatoes.

Beef à la Lindström

Biff à la Lindström

4 SERVINGS

4 TABLESPOONS (1/4 CUP) DRY
BREADCRUMBS
2 DL (3/4 CUP) WATER
1/2–1 TEASPOON SALT
1/4 TEASPOON GROUND BLACK PEPPER
400 G (14 OZ) GROUND BEEF
1 EGG
2 TABLESPOONS MINCED PICKLED BEET
2 TABLESPOONS MINCED ONION
1 TABLESPOON CAPERS
BUTTER

Soak breadcrumbs in water. Add salt
and pepper and let swell 10 minutes.
Add meat, egg, beet, onion and capers.
Combine lightly. Do not overwork.

Form 12 patties. Fry in butter until
golden brown and cooked through.

Serve with oven-roasted potatoes and
parsley butter.

Lindström is one of the most popular Swedish
surnames. There are still arguments about
which historical Lindström gave his name
to this classic Swedish dish.

Cold lemon soufflé

Citronfromage

4 SERVINGS

3 GELATIN SHEETS
3 EGGS
1 DL (SCANT 1/2 CUP) SUGAR
FINELY GRATED ZEST AND JUICE OF
1 LEMON
SLICED ALMONDS

Soak gelatin sheets in cold water to
soften, about 5 minutes.

Separate eggs. Beat egg yolks with sugar
until light and lemon-colored. Add
lemon zest and juice. Squeeze excess
water from gelatin sheets and melt in
a double boiler. Make sure there are no
lumps. Whisk into egg yolk mixture.

Beat egg whites until stiff and carefully
fold into egg yolk mixture.

Coat a bowl or individual dishes with
sugar. Pour in mixture and refrigerate
until set, about 2 1/2–3 hours.

Just before serving, garnish with sliced
almonds.

SKÄRSÅ, HÄLSINGLAND

Sour baltic herring

Surströmming

This dish is a Norrland specialty.
Baltic herring are salted and then left
to ferment. All that fermentation makes
the tins expand, and some do eventually
explode. The object is to open them
and savor the contents just before they
reach that point.

SOUR BALTIC HERRING
BUTTER
HARD FLATBREAD
COLD BOILED ALMOND POTATOES, SLICED
CHOPPED RED ONION
CRÈME FRAICHE

Bone and fillet fish. Butter bread, top
with sliced potatoes and sprinkle with
chopped onion. Top with sour herring
fillets. If flavor experience is too
intense, drizzle with crème fraiche.

This just may be the worst smelling dish in the
world. A northern Swedish dish with fermented
herring (source of odor) which is eaten with
crispbread, butter, onion and potatoes.

Jellied veal with beets

Kalvsylta med rödbetor

6–8 SERVINGS

1 KG (2 1/4 LB) SALTED VEAL SHOULDER
(FRESH VEAL CAN BE USED, BUT SALT
MUST BE ADDED TO BROTH)
2 ONIONS
2 CARROTS
15 CM (7") LENGTH LEEK
8 WHITE PEPPERCORNS
2 BAY LEAVES
1 DL (SCANT 1/2 CUP) PARSLEY LEAVES
(NO STALKS)
1 GELATIN SHEET
SALT AND FRESHLY GROUND PEPPER
JUICE OF 1/2 LEMON
1 DL (1/3 CUP) BALSAMIC VINEGAR
3 TABLESPOONS SUGAR
2 FRESH BOILED BEETS

Place meat in a heavy pot, add cold
water to cover and bring to a boil.
Drain, rinse meat and clean pot. This
helps to keep stock clear. Return meat
to pot, add cold water to cover and
bring to a boil. Add vegetables and
spices and simmer about 1 hour, until
meat is tender. Place meat under
pressure overnight.

Trim meat of fat and membrane, then
cut into thin slices. Shred parsley and
combine with meat.

Reduce cooking liquid until cloudy.
Soak gelatin sheet in cold water about
5 minutes to soften, then melt in hot
cooking liquid. Add salt, pepper and
lemon juice. Cool slightly, then pour
over meat to cover. Pour into individual
molds or into a 2-liter (8 cup) loaf pan
lined with plastic wrap. Refrigerate,
under light pressure, 24 hours.

Reduce vinegar and sugar until half
original amount remains. Carefully
slice jellied meat. Thinly slice beets.
Arrange on plates and drizzle with
balsamic vinegar syrup. There will
be leftover syrup, but it is difficult to
make a smaller batch.

Wallenbergers

Wallenbergare

4 SERVINGS

400 G (14 OZ) GROUND VEAL
2 DL (3/4 CUP) WHIPPING CREAM
4 EGG YOLKS
I TEASPOON SALT
1/4 TEASPOON FRESHLY GROUND
WHITE PEPPER
BREADCRUMBS
2 TABLESPOONS BUTTER

All ingredients should be very cold.
Place meat in a bowl. Gradually add
cream, mixing lightly. Add egg yolks,
one at a time, mixing lightly after each.
Add salt and pepper. Form into 8 patties
on a rinsed cutting board. Dip in breadcrumbs, then fry, over low heat, about
3 minutes per side, until golden and
puffed.

Serve with mashed potatoes, tiny peas
and melted butter.

The Wallenberg family is one of the richest
in Sweden. These Wallenberg patties are one
of the richest meat dishes in the Swedish
kitchen.

ART GLASS BY ULRIKA HYDMAN-VALLIEN, KOSTA BODA, ÅFORS

Peppermint candy

Polkagrisar

ABOUT 1/2 KILO (1 LB)

1/2 KG (1 LB) SUGAR
2 1/2 DL (1 CUP) WATER
1 TABLESPOON GLUCOSE
1 TEASPOON VINEGAR
2−3 DROPS PEPPERMINT OIL
RED FOOD COLORING

Combine sugar, water, glucose and
vinegar in a saucepan. Let stand at
least two hours, until sugar is partially
dissolved. Quickly bring to a boil, remove from heat and cool in pan. Pour
about 3/4 of the syrup onto an oiled
baking sheet and add peppermint oil.
Fold sides over toward the center using
an oiled knife or spatula so mixture
does not solidify unevenly. Work with
knife or spatula until mixture can be
handled. Using oiled hands, fold and
pull mixture.

Color remaining syrup with red food
coloring and pour in a thin stripe on an
oiled baking sheet. Divide red stripe in
two vertically and place a length on
each side of the white mixture. Twist
lengths together and cut into small,
even chunks with an oiled scissors.

This red and white candy from Gränna attracts
tourists from around the world. Peppermints
come in all shapes and sizes. Translated
literally from the Swedish, these are called
"polka pigs". They don't look at all like pigs,
but if you eat too many of them, you will start
to resemble one.

38

Cinnamon rolls and black currant juice

Kanelbullar och svartvinbärssaft

ABOUT 36–40 ROLLS

Rolls:
100 G (3 1/2 OZ) UNSALTED BUTTER
5 DL (2 CUPS) MILK
50 G (1 3/4 OZ) FRESH YEAST
1/2 TEASPOON SALT
1–1 1/2 DL (1/2–2/3 CUP) SUGAR
1 TEASPOON GROUND CARDAMOM
ABOUT 13 DL (5 1/2 CUPS) ALL-PURPOSE
FLOUR

Filling:
100 G (3 1/2 OZ) UNSALTED BUTTER,
SOFTENED
1 DL (SCANT 1/2 CUP) SUGAR
2 TABLESPOONS GROUND CINNAMON

Garnish:
1 EGG
PEARL SUGAR OR CRUSHED SUGAR CUBES

Melt butter, add milk and heat to 37°C (98°F).

Crumble yeast in a large bowl. Add some of milk mixture and stir until yeast is dissolved. Add remaining liquid, salt, sugar, cardamom and around 2/3 of the flour. Knead until smooth and elastic. Add more flour but save some for rolling out. Dough is ready when it begins to clean bowl. Sprinkle with flour. Cover and let rise in a warm place until doubled, about 30 minutes.

Knead dough a few minutes in bowl. Turn out onto a floured board. Knead in remaining flour. Dough is ready when it begins to clean board.

Roll out dough into a rectangle. Spread with soft butter, sprinkle with sugar and cinnamon and roll up. Cut into 1–2 cm (3/4") slices and place on greased baking sheets. Cover and let rise in a warm place until doubled, about 30 minutes.

Preheat oven to 250°C (475°F). Brush rolls with beaten egg and sprinkle with pearl sugar. Bake 5–10 minutes. Cool covered.

Black currant juice
ABOUT 4 LITERS (1 GALLON)

3 KG (6 1/2 LB) BLACK CURRANTS,
ABOUT 6 LITERS (QUARTS)
1 LITER (QUART) WATER
6 DL (2 1/2 CUPS) SUGAR PER LITER
(QUART) JUICE
SCANT 1/4 TEASPOON SODIUM BENZOATE
PER LITER (QUART) JUICE
SCANT 1/4 TEASPOON POTASSIUM SORBATE
PER LITER (QUART) JUICE

Clean and rinse berries. Bring water to a boil in a large pot. Add berries, cover and boil about 10 minutes. Now and then, press berries against side of pot to crush.

Pour berries into a straining cloth and let juice run off (do not press) for about 30 minutes. Measure juice. Clean pot and return juice to pot. Bring to a boil, add sugar, then bring to a boil once more. Skim well. Remove from heat. Stir sodium benzoate and potassium sorbate into a small amount of hot juice, then stir into pot.

Pour juice into clean bottles and seal while juice is still hot.

This rich, tangy juice is usually served diluted. Pour some into a glass, then add cold water to desired concentration.

Sweden has a coffee culture. Drinking coffee, preferably with something sweet alongside, is part of the Swedish lifestyle. And nothing tastes better with a cup of strong coffee than these cinnamon rolls.

Salmon casserole
with dill butter

Laxpudding med dillsmör

4 SERVINGS

600 G (1 1/3 LB) POTATOES BOILED
IN THEIR SKINS
1 SMALL ONION
BUTTER
400 G (14 OZ) SALTED OR MARINATED
SALMON
FRESHLY GROUND WHITE PEPPER
CHOPPED DILL
4 DL (1 2/3 CUPS) HALF AND HALF
3 EGGS

Preheat oven to 175°C (350°F). Peel and
slice potatoes. Chop onion and sweat in
a little butter until soft and transparent.
Dry salmon with paper towels and cut
into thin slices. Sprinkle with pepper.

In a 2 1/2 liter (10 cup) ovenproof dish,
layer potatoes and salmon, sprinkling
each layer with chopped dill and onion.
First and last layers should be potatoes.

Whisk together half and half and eggs
and season with pepper. Pour over
salmon and potatoes. Dot with butter.
Bake 45–60 minutes.

Serve with melted butter or dill butter.

Dill butter:
80 G (3 OZ) BUTTER, SOFTENED
SALT AND FRESHLY GROUND
WHITE PEPPER
FINELY CHOPPED DILL

Beat butter until fluffy. Season with salt
and pepper, then add dill.

Strawberry compote

Jordgubbskräm

4 SERVINGS

5–7 1/2 DL (2–3 CUPS) FRESH
STRAWBERRIES
5 DL (2 CUPS) WATER
3/4–1 DL (1/3–1/2 CUP) SUGAR
2 1/2 TABLESPOONS POTATO STARCH OR
CORNSTARCH

Clean strawberries. Cut large ones in
half or slice. Combine all ingredients
in a saucepan. Bring to a boil, stirring
carefully. Pour into a serving bowl.
Sprinkle with sugar to prevent a skin
from forming. Cool.

Substitute other juicy berries, such as
raspberries, blueberries or red currants
for strawberries.

Serve lukewarm or cold with milk.

Strawberry cream cake

Jordgubbstårta

ABOUT 10 SERVINGS

Sponge layers:
4 EGGS
2 DL (3/4 CUP) SUGAR
1 DL (1/2 CUP) ALL-PURPOSE FLOUR
1 DL (1/3 CUP) POTATO STARCH OR
CORNSTARCH
2 TEASPOONS BAKING POWDER

Preheat oven to 175°C (350°F). Grease and flour 25 cm (10") springform pan.

Beat eggs and sugar until thick, light and lemon-colored. Sift together dry ingredients and carefully fold into egg mixture. Pour into prepared pan. Bake on lowest oven shelf 35 minutes. Cool 10 minutes before removing from pan. Place on rack and cover until completely cool.

Filling:
1 1/2 LITERS (6 CUPS) FRESH
STRAWBERRIES
2 TABLESPOONS SUGAR
1 BANANA
4 DL (1 2/3 CUPS) WHIPPING CREAM
2 TABLESPOONS APRICOT MARMALADE
(SMOOTH)

Divide sponge cake into two layers. Mash 1/2 liter (2 cups) strawberries with sugar and banana. Spread on one layer. Top with second layer.

Lightly whip cream and spread over entire cake, even around the sides. Halve or slice remaining strawberries and arrange on top.

Melt marmalade in microwave and brush over strawberries for a shiny finish.

Three sandwiches

Tre sandvikare

8 SERVINGS

Shrimp:
4 THIN SLICES WHITE BREAD
4 TABLESPOONS (1/4 CUP) MAYONNAISE
2 HARD-COOKED EGGS
24 PEELED SHRIMP
DILL SPRIGS

Halve bread slices or cut out circles
with a round cookie cutter.

Spread a thick layer of mayonnaise
on each piece of bread. Quarter eggs
lengthwise and place two quarters on
each round of bread. Arrange shrimp
over egg and decorate with dill sprigs.

Cheese:
4 THIN SLICES DARK RYE BREAD
200 G (7 OZ) BLUE CHEESE, CUT INTO
8 SLICES OF EQUAL SIZE
1/2 PEAR
2 RADISHES

Halve bread slices or cut out circles
with a round cookie cutter.

Place a slice of cheese on each piece
of bread. Cut pear into sticks and place
on cheese. Thinly slice radishes and
sprinkle over cheese.

Meat:
2 TEASPOONS GRATED FRESH
HORSERADISH
4 TABLESPOONS (2 OZ) LIGHT
CREAM CHEESE
4 THIN SLICES LIGHT RYE BREAD
8 THIN SLICES SMOKED REINDEER
OR BEEF
CHIVES

Combine horseradish and cream cheese.

Halve bread slices or cut out circles
with a round cookie cutter.

Spread horseradish-cheese on each
piece of bread. Loosely fold meat
and place two slices on each piece
of bread. Garnish with chives.

Anchovies

Ansjovis

Swedish anchovies are herring which
are layered with a mixture of sugar,
salt and spices directly into cans or
into large wooden barrels. After four
to six weeks, the herring have been
transformed into delicious anchovies.

Mock anchovies:
600 G (1 1/3 LB) BALTIC (OR OTHER)
HERRING FILLETS, GUTTED AND CLEANED
(ABOUT 1 KG (2 1/4 LB) WHOLE)
SALT
1–1 1/2 DL (1/2–2/3 CUP) OIL
3–4 TABLESPOONS VINEGAR
2 TABLESPOONS KETCHUP
1 DL (1/2 CUP) FINELY CHOPPED DILL
1 1/2 TABLESPOONS SUGAR
SALT
4 DROPS TABASCO

Preheat oven to 175°C (350°F).

Cut off back fins and rinse well. Salt fish
inside. Layer in an ovenproof dish, back
facing up. Combine remaining
ingredients and pour over fish. Bake
about 30 minutes. Cool slightly.

Serve fish lukewarm or cold, with boiled
potatoes and crispbread.

Swedish hash

Pytt i panna

4 SERVINGS

10–12 COLD BOILED POTATOES
2 ONIONS
BUTTER
300 G (10 OZ) MEAT (BRISKET, VEAL
OR FRIED BACON AND SAUSAGE)
SALT AND PEPPER
4 EGGS

Peel and cube potatoes. Chop onions
and cube meat. Fry potatoes and onions
in butter until golden brown. Set aside.
Brown meat on all sides. Fold in potato
mixture and season with salt and pepper.
Heat through.

Fry eggs in butter, sunny side up.

Arrange mounds of hash on each
plate. Top with a fried egg. Serve
with Worcestershire sauce, HP sauce,
pickled beets and pickles.

Hard rye crispbread

Hårt rågbröd

ABOUT 25 SHEETS

50 G (1 3/4 OZ) FRESH YEAST
1 LITER (QUART) WARM WATER (37°C, 98°F)
5 TEASPOONS SALT
4 TEASPOONS CRUSHED FENNEL
1 1/2 LITERS (6 1/4 CUPS) COARSE
RYE FLOUR
1 1/2 LITERS (6 1/4 CUPS) ALL-PURPOSE
FLOUR

Crumble yeast into water and stir until
dissolved. Add remaining ingredients,
setting aside a little flour for rolling.
Knead until smooth and elastic. Let
rest about 30 minutes.

Roll out to 1 mm (as thinly as possible).
Cut around a dish to make circles.
Or divide dough into 25 pieces of equal
size. Roll out each until very thin.
Prick with special rolling pin or fork.
Let rise 30 minutes.

Bake on a hot griddle (200°C, 400°F) on
one side only, about 10 minutes. Cool
on a rack.

Lingonberry compote

Rårörda lingon

ABOUT 2 1/2 LITERS (10 CUPS)

2 KG (ABOUT 3 LITERS (12 CUPS)
LINGONBERRIES
1 1/2 LITER (6 CUPS) SUGAR

Clean and rinse berries. Place in a large bowl. Add sugar and stir until sugar is dissolved and berries are crushed. Pour into clean, cold glass jars. Seal.

It is possible to freeze small batches of lingonberries and make compote as needed.

This fresh compote can be frozen, but it develops a sharp flavor if stored longer than 3–4 months.

Saffron pancakes

Saffranspannkaka

8 SERVINGS

1/2 DL (3 1/2 TABLESPOONS) LONG-GRAIN
RICE
1 DL (SCANT 1/2 CUP) WATER
4 DL (1 2/3 CUPS) MILK
3 DL (1 1/4 CUPS) WHIPPING CREAM
1 TABLESPOON BUTTER
SCANT 1/4 TEASPOON SALT
1 G (1 TEASPOON) SAFFRON
(THREADS PACKED)
2 TABLESPOONS COGNAC
3 TABLESPOONS HONEY
1/4 TEASPOON CINNAMON
1/2 TEASPOON GROUND CARDAMOM
50 G (1/2 CUP) FINELY-CHOPPED ALMONDS
4 EGGS
1 TABLESPOON ALL-PURPOSE FLOUR
2 TABLESPOONS MILK

Add rice to water and simmer until most water has evaporated. Add milk and cream. Simmer until rice is very soft, about 40 minutes. Stir in butter and salt. Combine saffron, cognac, honey, cinnamon, cardamom and nuts and add. Preheat oven to 200°C (400°F).

Whisk eggs, flour and milk and add to rice mixture. Pour into a greased ovenproof dish and bake on lowest oven shelf about 20 minutes.
Serve pancake warm with whipped cream and berries or jam.

Cloudberry soup

Hjortronsoppa

4 SERVINGS

400 G (14 OZ) CLOUDBERRIES
1 DL (1/2 CUP) SUGAR
2 DL (3/4 CUP) WHITE WINE
5 DL (2 CUPS) WATER
1/2 DL (3 1/2 TABLESPOONS) FRESH
LEMON JUICE
1/2 DL (3 1/2 TABLESPOONS) FRESH
ORANGE JUICE
1 CINNAMON STICK
1/2 VANILLA BEAN
1–1 1/2 TABLESPOONS CORNSTARCH
STIRRED INTO 1 TABLESPOON COLD WATER

Clean berries. Melt sugar in a heavy saucepan. Carefully add berries and liquids. Bring to a boil, then remove half the berries with a slotted spoon and save for garnish. Add spices and simmer slowly 15 minutes. Thicken with cornstarch mixture. Strain off spices and any berries which have disintegrated. Add reserved berries.

Serve cold or warm with vanilla ice cream.

Punch torte

Punschtårta

ABOUT 8 PIECES

4 EGGS
1 1/2 DL (2/3 CUP) SUGAR
1 1/2 DL (2/3 CUP) ALL-PURPOSE FLOUR
1 TEASPOON BAKING POWDER
1 DL (SCANT 1/2 CUP) WATER
1/2 DL (3 1/2 TABLESPOONS) SUGAR
2 DL (3/4 CUP) PUNCH (ARRAK-FLAVORED
SWEDISH LIQUEUR)
2 DL (3/4 CUP) WHIPPING CREAM
100 G (3 1/2 OZ) BITTERSWEET CHOCOLATE

Preheat oven to 200°C (400°F). Grease and flour a 22 cm (9") springform pan.

Beat eggs and sugar until thick, light and lemon-colored. Combine flour and baking powder and fold in lightly. Pour into prepared pan. Bake 25 minutes.

Bring water and sugar to a boil. Remove from heat and add punch. Pour over cake. Refrigerate.

Just before serving, whip cream and spread over cake. Using a potato peeler, cut shreds of chocolate and sprinkle over tart.

Rusks

Skorpor

ABOUT 100

175 G (6 OZ) UNSALTED BUTTER
5 DL (2 CUPS) MILK
50 G (1 3/4 OZ) FRESH YEAST
1/2 TEASPOON SALT
1 1/2 DL (2/3 CUP) SUGAR
2 TEASPOONS GROUND CARDAMOM
1 TEASPOON BAKING POWDER (IF DESIRED)
1 1/3 LITERS (5 1/4 CUPS) ALL-PURPOSE
FLOUR

Melt butter, add milk and heat to 37°C (98°F).

Crumble yeast into some of milk mixture and stir until dissolved. Add remaining liquid, salt, sugar, cardamom, and baking powder (if desired, to make rusks extra crisp). Knead in enough flour to make a smooth and elastic dough. Sprinkle with flour, cover and let rise in a warm place 30–40 minutes.

Knead in remaining flour, first in bowl, then on a floured board. Form into 50 round rolls. Place on greased baking sheets. Cover and let rise in a warm place about 30 minutes.

Preheat oven to 225°C (425°F). Bake 10 minutes on center oven shelf. Cool, uncovered, on a rack.

Lower oven to 185°C (375°F). Halve rolls with a fork or bread knife. Bake until golden, about 5 minutes.

Lower oven to 100°C (210°F). Dry rusks in oven about 2 hours. Leave oven door slightly open during drying process. It is possible to dry two sheets of rusks at a time, but switch them around after half the drying time.

49

TÄNNFORS RAPIDS, JÄMTLAND

Salt beef with autumn vegetable gratin

Tjälknöl och gratinerade höströtter

12 SERVINGS

1 1/2–2 KG (3–4 1/2 LB) MOOSE OR BEEF
RUMP ROAST, FROZEN SOLID
1 LITER (QUART) WATER
1 DL (SCANT 1/2 CUP) NON-IODIZED SALT
1 TABLESPOON SUGAR
1 TEASPOON CRUSHED BLACK
PEPPERCORNS
8 COARSELY CRUSHED JUNIPER BERRIES
1 TEASPOON ROSEMARY
1 CRUMBLED BAY LEAF

Place frozen meat in an ovenproof glass dish and turn oven temperature to 75°C (170°F). Roast until internal temperature reaches 64°C (147°F).

Combine remaining ingredients and heat until salt and sugar are dissolved. Place meat in a doubled plastic bag and add salt brine. Seal bag and marinate about 5 hours.

Remove meat and cut into thin slices. Serve with vegetable gratin. Thin slices of salt beef are delicious in sandwiches.

Autumn vegetable gratin
12 SERVINGS

8 CARROTS
1 CELERIAC
4 PARSNIPS
1 RUTABAGA
1 1/2 KG (3 LB) POTATOES
3 GARLIC CLOVES, MINCED
13 TWIGS THYME
4 DL (1 2/3 CUPS) CRÈME FRAICHE OR
DAIRY SOUR CREAM
SALT AND FRESHLY GROUND WHITE PEPPER
300 G (2 1/2 CUPS) GRATED AGED CHEESE,
SUCH AS SWISS

Preheat oven to 200°C (400°F).

Peel and slice vegetables. Bring a pot of salted water to a boil. Blanch carrots, celeriac and parsnips together. Remove with slotted spoon and drain. Cook rutabaga separately. It takes longer. Potatoes need no blanching. Chop garlic. Peel thyme leaves off twigs and shred. Combine crème fraiche with garlic, thyme, salt and pepper and fold into vegetable mixture. Fold half the cheese into vegetable mixture, then pour into an ovenproof dish. Top with remaining cheese. Bake 30 minutes.

This dish was an accident. A woman put a frozen roast into the oven at 70°C (160°F) – to defrost it – and asked her husband to remove it after a few hours. He forgot and the roast was in the oven overnight.

Seven kinds of cookies

Sju sorters kakor

Caramel cookies
ABOUT 40 COOKIES

200 G (7 OZ) UNSALTED BUTTER, SOFTENED
1 1/2 DL (2/3 CUP) SUGAR
2 TABLESPOONS GOLDEN SYRUP OR
GOLDEN MOLASSES
2 TEASPOONS BAKING POWDER
2 TEASPOONS VANILLA EXTRACT
6 DL (1 2/3 CUPS) ALL-PURPOSE FLOUR

Preheat oven to 200°C (400°F). Line
a baking sheet with baking parchment.
Combine all ingredients. Form dough
into three long rolls, flatten and place
on parchment. Bake around 8 minutes,
until golden brown. Remove from
oven and cut on the diagonal into 3 cm
(1 1/4") slices. Cool.

Dreams
ABOUT 60 COOKIES

200 G (7 OZ) UNSALTED BUTTER, SOFTENED
1 1/2 DL (2/3 CUP) SUGAR
1 3/4 TEASPOONS VANILLA EXTRACT
1/2 TEASPOON HORNSALT (AMMONIUM
CARBONATE) OR 1 1/2 TEASPOONS BAKING
POWDER
5 DL (2 1/4 CUPS) ALL-PURPOSE FLOUR

Preheat oven to 150°C (300°F). Line
a baking sheet with baking parchment.
Beat butter, sugar and vanilla until
light and fluffy. Dissolve hornsalt in
1 teaspoon water and add. Add flour
and knead until smooth. Divide dough
into three equal parts and make 20 balls
from each. Place on parchment and
press each cookie lightly with a wet
finger. Bake about 20 minutes.

Chocolate slices
ABOUT 80 COOKIES

5 DL (2 1/4 CUPS) ALL-PURPOSE FLOUR
2 1/2 DL (1 CUP) SUGAR
4 TABLESPOONS (1/4 CUP) UNSWEETENED
COCOA
1 TEASPOON BAKING POWDER
1 1/2 TEASPOONS VANILLA EXTRACT
200 G (7 OZ) UNSALTED BUTTER, SOFTENED
2 EGGS
PEARL SUGAR OR CRUSHED SUGAR CUBES

Preheat oven to 200°C (400°F). Line
a baking sheet with baking parchment.
Combine dry ingredients. Knead in
vanilla, butter and 1 egg until smooth.
Divide dough into six equal parts and
form into finger-thick lengths. Place on
parchment and flatten. Lightly beat
remaining egg. Brush on dough, then
sprinkle with pearl sugar.

Bake about 15 minutes. Cool, then cut
on the diagonal into 3 cm (1 1/4") slices.

Nut logs
ABOUT 40 COOKIES

200 G (7 OZ) UNSALTED BUTTER, SOFTENED
1 DL (1/2 CUP) SUGAR
100 G (3 1/2 OZ, 1 CUP) FINELY CHOPPED
OR GROUND HAZELNUTS
3 1/2 DL (1 1/2 CUPS) ALL-PURPOSE FLOUR
CHOPPED HAZELNUTS

Preheat oven to 200°C (400°F). Line
a baking sheet with baking parchment.
Beat butter and sugar until light and
fluffy. Knead in nuts and flour until
smooth. Divide dough into four parts
and roll each into a finger-thick roll.
Place on parchment and divide each
roll into 10 lengths. Flatten lightly with
fingers and sprinkle with chopped
hazelnuts. Bake about 12 minutes.

Jam thumbprints
ABOUT 30 COOKIES

150 G (5 1/2 OZ) UNSALTED BUTTER,
SOFTENED
1/2 DL (3 1/2 TABLESPOONS) SUGAR
1 EGG YOLK
1 TEASPOON VANILLA EXTRACT
3 DL (1 1/4 CUPS) ALL-PURPOSE FLOUR
3 TABLESPOONS RASPBERRY OR
STRAWBERRY JAM

Preheat oven to 200°C (400°F). Line
a baking sheet with baking parchment.
Beat butter and sugar until light and
fluffy. Add egg yolk and vanilla. Quickly
knead in flour. Divide dough into two
15 cm (6") long rolls. Wrap in plastic
and refrigerate until hard. Cut into
1 cm (1/2") slices and place on lined
sheet. Press thumb gently in center
of each. Place a small amount of jam
in each thumbprint. Bake 5–7 minutes,
until golden brown.

Checkerboard cookies
ABOUT 60 COOKIES

200 G (7 OZ) UNSALTED BUTTER, SOFTENED
1 DL (SCANT 1/2 CUP) SUGAR
5 DL (2 CUPS) ALL-PURPOSE FLOUR
2 TABLESPOONS UNSWEETENED COCOA

Preheat oven to 200°C (400°F). Line
a baking sheet with baking parchment.
Beat butter and sugar until light and
fluffy. Knead in flour until smooth.
Divide dough into two equal parts.
Add cocoa to one part and knead until
evenly colored. Form two white rolls
and two brown rolls. Place one white
and one brown roll next to each other.
Place a brown roll on the white and
a white roll on the brown to form a
checkerboard. Press top and sides to
form a "brick". Refrigerate one hour.

Cut into 1–1 1/2 cm (1/2–3/4") slices
and place on lined sheet. Bake 5–7
minutes. Cool on a rack.

Oatmeal cookies
ABOUT 60 COOKIES

6 DL (2 1/2 CUPS) ROLLED OATS
3 DL (1 1/4 CUPS) SUGAR
2 DL (3/4 CUP) ALL-PURPOSE FLOUR
1 1/2 TEASPOONS BAKING POWDER
200 G (7 OZ) UNSALTED BUTTER, SOFTENED
2 1/2 DL (1 CUP) RAISINS

Preheat oven to 200°C (400°F). Line
a baking sheet with baking parchment.
Combine dry ingredients. Work in
butter. Coarsely chop raisins and add.
Mix until smooth. Form small balls and
place on parchment. Bake on center
oven shelf about 12 minutes.

Swedes love coffee (second largest consumers
of coffee in the world) – and sweets. The
tradition of serving "seven kinds of cookies"
at a coffee party developed during the 1800s.

Marinated salmon with mustard sauce

Gravad lax med senapssås

10 SERVINGS

1 KG (2 1/4 LB) SALMON, PREFERABLY
CENTER SECTION OF ONE FILLET, FRESH
AND OF THE HIGHEST QUALITY (BEST
IN THE SPRING)
2 TEASPOONS VEGETABLE OIL
4 TABLESPOONS (1/4 CUP) SUGAR
2 TABLESPOONS SALT
1 TEASPOON CRUSHED WHITE
PEPPERCORNS
1 LARGE BUNCH DILL (WITH STALKS),
CHOPPED

Scale fish. Wipe with paper towels.
Ask fishmonger to remove bones, or
draw finger down thickest part of fillet
to locate bones. Remove with tweezers.
Remove fat, but do not remove skin.
Rub fillet with oil. Combine sugar,
salt and pepper and rub into fish.

Place half of chopped dill in a glass dish
just large enough to hold fish. Place fish
in dish, skin side up. Top with remaining
dill. Cover with a small cutting board
and place a weight on top, to weigh
down fish lightly. Refrigerate 12–24
hours. Turn fish several times. If fish
marinates too long, it becomes hard.

Scrape off seasonings and cut into
thin slices on the diagonal, or into 3 cm
(1 1/4) thick straight slices. Do not cut
through skin. If desired, skin can be
cut into 1 cm (1/2") strips and fried in
oil as garnish.

Any pink fish, such as char or trout,
can be used in this recipe.

Mustard sauce
1 TABLESPOON MILD, SWEET SWEDISH
MUSTARD
1 TABLESPOON DARK FRENCH MUSTARD
1/2 TABLESPOON HONEY
1 TABLESPOON RED WINE VINEGAR
SALT AND FRESHLY GROUND WHITE
PEPPER
2 DL (3/4 CUP) VEGETABLE OIL
(NOT OLIVE OIL)
CHOPPED DILL

Whisk together mustards, honey and
vinegar. Season with salt and pepper.
Whisk in oil in a thin stream until
emulsified. Stir in dill and correct
seasoning.

400 years ago, large catches of salmon
were buried in salt for preservation.
The Swedish name for this dish, *gravad lax*,
refers to that method.

MAKING DALA HORSES, NUSNÄS, DALARNA

Marinated herring

Inlagd sill

4 SERVINGS

8 PRESOAKED SALT HERRING FILLETS

Brine:
3 DL (1 1/2 CUPS) 7% VINEGAR
1 DL (1/2 CUP) WATER
2 DL (1 CUP) SUGAR
2 ONIONS, SLICED
1 TEASPOON CRUSHED WHITE
PEPPERCORNS
2 TEASPOONS CRUSHED ALLSPICE BERRIES

Garnish:
1 RED ONION, SLICED
2 CARROTS, SHREDDED
3 CM (1 1/4") CUBE FRESH HORSERADISH,
SHREDDED
2 BAY LEAVES

Remove all small bones from fillets.
Rinse well under cold running water.

Combine ingredients in brine and bring
to a boil. Cool.

Cut fillets on the diagonal into
2 cm (3/4") slices and place in a jar.
Add brine and refrigerate at least
24 hours. Garnish with onion, carrots,
horseradish and bay leaves.

For a large quantity of herring, leave
fillets whole and place in a large jar.
Just before serving, cut into slices
and garnish with fresh vegetables and
crushed spices. Drizzle a little brine
on top.

No other food is so closely associated with
the Swedish summer as herring. Marinated
herring, served cold, is always eaten with
boiled new potatoes, sour cream and chives.

Blueberry pie with vanilla sauce

Blåbärspaj med vaniljsås

6 SERVINGS

200 G (7 OZ) UNSALTED BUTTER
I DL (I/2 CUP) SUGAR
2 DL (3/4 CUP) GOLDEN SYRUP
6 DL (2 I/2 CUPS) ROLLED OATS
2 DL (3/4 CUP) ALL-PURPOSE FLOUR
4 TABLESPOONS (I/4 CUP) WHIPPING
CREAM
4 DL (I 2/3 CUPS) BLUEBERRIES
2 TABLESPOONS SUGAR
2 TABLESPOONS CORNSTARCH

Preheat oven to 175°C (350°F). Melt
butter and add sugar and syrup. Stir
in oats, flour and cream. Sprinkle half
of oat mixture in a pie pan. Top with
berries, then sprinkle with remaining
oat mixture. Bake about 20 minutes.
Serve lukewarm or cold with vanilla
sauce.

Vanilla sauce:
I VANILLA BEAN
3 DL (I I/4 CUPS) MILK
3 EGG YOLKS
2 TABLESPOONS SUGAR
3 EGG YOLKS
2 DL (3/4 CUP) WHIPPING CREAM

Split vanilla bean lengthwise and
scrape out seeds. Combine bean, seeds
and milk in a heavy saucepan (not
aluminum, as it discolors eggs) and
bring to a boil. Whisk together egg yolks
and sugar. Whisk in hot vanilla milk.
Clean milk pan and return mixture to
pan. Simmer over low heat, stirring
constantly, until mixture begins to
thicken. Place pan in cold water and
whisk until cold. Strain or remove
vanilla bean. Refrigerate. Just before
serving, whip cream and fold into sauce.
Serve sauce chilled with warm pie.

LOBSTER FISHING, KÄRINGÖN, BOHUSLÄN

Poached cod with egg, shrimp and horseradish

Pocherad torsk med ägg,
räkor och pepparrot

4 SERVINGS

4 COD STEAKS (ON THE BONE),
ABOUT 200 G (7 OZ) EACH

Court bouillon for fish:
2 LITERS (QUARTS) WATER
4 TABLESPOONS (1/4 CUP) SALT
1/2 ONION
1 BAY LEAF
4 WHITE PEPPERCORNS
2 ALLSPICE BERRIES

3 HARD-COOKED EGGS
200 G (7 OZ) SHELLED SHRIMP
100 G (3 1/2 OZ) UNSALTED BUTTER
1 CHUNK FRESH HORSERADISH, GRATED
1 DL (1/2 CUP) CHOPPED DILL
(DO NOT USE DRIED DILL)

Rinse fish in cold water, removing all
blood.

Bring court bouillon to a rolling boil,
add fish, and return to a boil. Place
a dish over fish slices to keep them
under water, cover and remove from
heat. After 6 minutes, fish should be
cooked through. Peel and chop eggs.
Chop shrimp. Melt butter.

Remove fish from water with a slotted
spoon, draining well, or drain on a
kitchen towel. Place on serving platter.

Reheat butter, add eggs, shrimp,
horseradish and dill. Spoon over fish.

Serve with boiled new potatoes or riced
potatoes.

Boiled lobster

Hummerkok

1 lobster per person as a main dish,
1/2 as an appetizer

6 LITERS (QUARTS) WATER
2 2/3 DL (1 HEAPING CUP) SALT
2 TEASPOONS CARAWAY SEED
2 SUGAR CUBES
2 LIVE LOBSTERS

In a medium pot, bring water to a boil,
then add salt, caraway seed and sugar.
Cook one lobster at a time. Plunge, head
first, into boiling water. Cook 1 minute
per 100 g (3 1/2 oz) after water returns
to a boil.

Remove lobster with slotted spoon and
cool in ice water. Remove from water
after cooling.

If lobsters are to be served the following
day, store in cooking liquid diluted with
water, so they don't absorb too much
salt. Do not put fingers in water, as
lobsters are sensitive to bacteria.

Serve lobsters cold with mayonnaise
and toast.

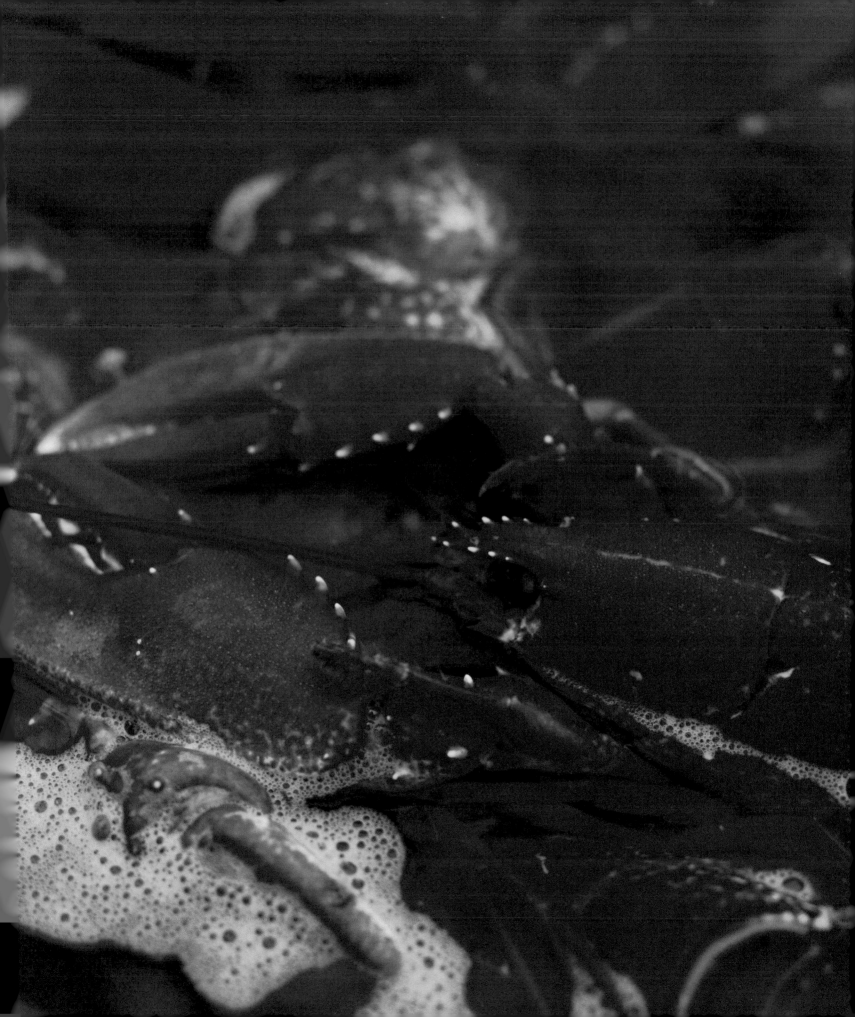

Toast Skagen

Toast Skagen

4 SERVINGS

400 G (14 OZ) PEELED SHRIMP
1/2 DL (3 1/2 TABLESPOONS) MAYONNAISE
1/2 DL (3 1/2 TABLESPOONS) CRÈME
FRAICHE
3 TABLESPOONS CHOPPED FRESH DILL
(DO NOT USE DRIED DILL)
1/2 TABLESPOON FRESH LEMON JUICE
SALT AND FRESHLY GROUND WHITE
PEPPER
4 SLICES WHITE BREAD
BUTTER
80–100 G (3–3 1/2 OZ) WHITEFISH CAVIAR
LEMON WEDGES
PEELED SHRIMP

Chop shrimp if large. Combine with
mayonnaise, crème fraiche, dill, lemon
juice, salt and pepper.

Sauté bread in butter until golden.

Divide shrimp mixture among bread
slices. Top with caviar and garnish with
lemon wedges and peeled shrimp.

The name comes from Sweden's neighbor,
Denmark. Skagen, at the northern tip of
Denmark, is a popular fishing port. Toast
Skagen is probably the most popular
appetizer in Sweden.

70

West coast salad with Rhode Island sauce

Västkustsallad med
Rhode Islandsås

4 SERVINGS

I COOKED LOBSTER OR CRAB
300 G (10 1/2 OZ) COOKED SHRIMP
15 COOKED MUSSELS
ABOUT 300 G (10 OZ) FRESH WHITE OR
GREEN ASPARAGUS
100 G (4 OZ) MIXED GREENS
10 SMALL CHERRY TOMATOES
150 G (5 OZ) FRESH MUSHROOMS
1/2 SNAKE CUCUMBER
3 TABLESPOONS VINAIGRETTE

Peel and clean shellfish. Save a few
mussels in their shells for garnish.
Cut lobster into small chunks.

Peel asparagus and cook in salted-
sugared water about 3 minutes.
Rinse mixed greens and pluck into
bite-size pieces. Halve tomatoes, slice
mushrooms and cube cucumber.

Arrange greens on a serving platter.
Combine seafood and half the vegetables
and mix with vinaigrette. Arrange on
greens. Arrange remaining vegetables
around shellfish and garnish with
mussels.

Serve with toast and a good dressing.

Rhode Island sauce:
3 DL (1 CUP) MAYONNAISE
I DL (1/3 CUP) NATURAL YOGURT
1/2 DL (3 TABLESPOONS) CHILE SAUCE
(SIMILAR TO KETCHUP)
1/2 TABLESPOON MADEIRA
SALT AND FRESHLY GROUND PEPPER

Combine all ingredients.

Rhode Island sauce is good with all
kinds of shellfish salads and cocktails.

Apple pie

Äppelpaj

4–5 SERVINGS

Pie crust:
3 DL (1 1/4 CUPS) ALL-PURPOSE FLOUR
125 G (4 OZ) UNSALTED BUTTER,
SOFTENED
2 TABLESPOONS WATER

Filling:
4–5 (ABOUT 600 G (1 1/3 LB) APPLES
2–3 TABLESPOONS SUGAR
1–2 TABLESPOONS CINNAMON
1/2–1 EGG, LIGHTLY BEATEN

Place flour in a bowl. Crumble butter into flour until consistency of large crumbs. Add water and mix quickly to form a light pastry. Or combine in a food processor until pastry cleans sides. Form pastry into a ball, cover with plastic wrap and refrigerate at least 1 hour.

Roll out about half the pastry and press into a greased 25 cm (10") pie pan.

Preheat oven to 225°C (425°F).

Peel and core apples. Cut into thin wedges and place in pie shell. Sprinkle with sugar and cinnamon.

Roll out remaining pastry to cover apples completely, overlapping sides by about 5 cm (2"). Fold under bottom crust to seal. Make slashes in top crust for steam to escape. Or, cut out strips for a latticework top crust. Brush with beaten egg.

Bake on lowest oven shelf about 35 minutes.

Roast eel

Luad ål

4 SERVINGS

I MEDIUM EEL
SALT
JUNIPER TWIGS

Sprinkle eel with salt and let marinate
6 hours. Preheat oven to 250°C (475°F).
Clean and scrape fish, but leave skin on.
Rinse and dry thoroughly with a towel.

Place chopped juniper twigs in an
oven pan and top with a rack. Place
eel on rack and bake until skin is dark
brown and crisp, about 30 minutes.
Turn several times while roasting for
an even color.

Serve eel whole with riced potatoes.

Beer-poached eel

Pilsnerkokt ål

4 SERVINGS

800 G (I 3/4 LB) FRESH EEL
2 BOTTLES BEER
I BAY LEAF
6 WHITE PEPPERCORNS
I TABLESPOON SALT

Clean, flay and rinse eel. Cut into
5 cm (2") long chunks. Combine
remaining ingredients and add eel.
Marinate 12 hours. Simmer in
marinade about 12 minutes.

Serve eel with creamed potatoes.

Smoked eel with scrambled eggs

Rökt ål med äggröra

4 SERVINGS

6 EGGS
I DL (I/3 CUP) WATER OR
WHIPPING CREAM (DO NOT USE MILK)
SALT AND BLACK PEPPER
BUTTER

4 SLICES WHOLE GRAIN BREAD
350 G (I2 OZ) FLAT-SMOKED EEL, SLICED
I TABLESPOON CHOPPED FRESH CHIVES

Break eggs into a bowl. Whisk lightly
with a fork, add water or cream, salt
and pepper. Heat butter in a heavy
skillet (not aluminum, which discolors
eggs). When butter begins to turn
brown, add eggs. Stir slowly until eggs
are creamy and semi-solid. Do not
allow to dry out. Stir in a pat of cold
butter, then remove from heat.

Serve on bread with smoked eel.
Sprinkle with chives.

Eel is eaten primarily in Skåne in the fall.
When the night is so dark that eel cannot
not see the nets, it's called "eel darkness".

Lingonberry parfait with almond tuiles

Lingonparfait med mandelflarn

8 SERVINGS

2 EGGS
1 3/4 DL (3/4 CUP) CONFECTIONER'S
SUGAR
3 DL (1 1/4 CUPS) WHIPPING CREAM
4 CL (3 TABLESPOONS) ABSOLUT VODKA
1 DL (SCANT 1/2 CUP) LINGONBERRY
PUREE
25 G (1/4 CUP) TOASTED SLICED ALMONDS
OR ALMOND TUILES

Whisk eggs and sugar over simmering water until thick. Remove from heat and continue whisking until cold.

Whip cream. Stir vodka into berry puree and stir into egg mixture. Fold in cream. Pour into a 1 1/2 liter (6 cups) round mold or loaf pan. Freeze at least 4 hours, preferably more.

Remove from freezer 15–30 minutes before serving. Dip mold into very hot water 30 seconds. Unmold. Cut into serving pieces. Garnish with sliced almonds or almond tuiles.

Almond tuiles:
(ABOUT 20 COOKIES)

100 G (3 1/2 OZ, ABOUT 2/3 CUP)
BLANCHED ALMONDS
100 G (3 1/2 OZ) UNSALTED BUTTER
1 DL (SCANT 1/2 CUP) SUGAR
2 TABLESPOONS ALL-PURPOSE FLOUR
2 TABLESPOONS MILK

Preheat oven to 200°C (400°F). Line a baking sheet with baking parchment.

Chop almonds, Melt butter and sugar in a saucepan over low heat. Combine flour with chopped almonds and stir in butter, then milk. Place spoonfuls of mixture far apart on prepared sheet. Bake 5–8 minutes, until cookies have spread out and turned golden.

It is important not to stir melted sugar and butter too much. This batter keeps up to five days in the refrigerator.

Lingonberries are called the "red gold of the forest" and are a key ingredient in the Swedish kitchen. They can be used as an accompaniment to main dishes, in jam or compotes and in desserts.

78

Crayfish soup with Västerbotten pie

Kräftsoppa med västerbottenpaj

8 CUPS OR 4 BOWLS

Soup:
800 G (1 3/4 LB) CRAYFISH SHELLS OR
1 KG (2 1/4 LB) COOKED CRAYFISH
1 SMALL CARROT
1/2 PARSNIP
4 CM (1 1/2") CUBE CELERIAC
4 SHALLOTS
2 GARLIC CLOVES
1 CHIPOTLE (SMOKED JALAPEÑO) CHILE,
OR 1 DRIED CHILE
50 G (3 TABLESPOONS) BUTTER
3 TABLESPOONS TOMATO PASTE
1 BOTTLE (3 CUPS) WHITE WINE
5 DL (2 CUPS) WATER
1 CAN (14 OZ) CHOPPED TOMATOES
2 STALKS FRESH TARRAGON
1 DILL CROWN OR 1 TEASPOON DILL SEED
2 DL (3/4 CUP) CRÈME FRAICHE
3 TABLESPOONS CORNSTARCH STIRRED
INTO 2 TABLESPOONS COLD WATER
SALT AND PEPPER
1/2 DL (3 TABLESPOONS) COGNAC OR
MADEIRA
1 TABLESPOON UNSALTED BUTTER

Pie crust:
100 G (3 1/2 OZ) SALTED BUTTER
3 DL (1 1/4 CUPS) ALL-PURPOSE FLOUR
2 1/2 TABLESPOONS WATER

OR 500 G (1 LB) PUFF PASTRY

Pie filling:
2 DL (1 CUP) CRÈME FRAICHE
2 DL (2/3 CUP) MILK
3 EGGS
2 EGG YOLKS
150 G (5 OZ, 1 1/4 CUPS) VÄSTERBOTTEN
(OR OTHER FLAVORFUL) CHEESE
SALT AND PEPPER

Garnish:
200 G (7 OZ) CRAYFISH TAILS AND,
IF DESIRED, 8 CRAYFISH

Soup:
Save any liquid from crayfish to season soup.

Remove stomach, just behind head of crayfish, as it can make soup bitter.

Peel carrot, parsnip and celeriac and cut into 2 cm (3/4") cubes. Slice shallots. Mince garlic and chile. Heat a heavy saucepan and add butter. Sauté vegetables until golden, add crayfish shells and sauté until all liquid has been released and evaporated. Add tomato paste, then liquid. Simmer slowly 30 minutes, adding additional water to keep shells covered. Add crushed tomatoes and tarragon. Chop dill crowns and add. Bring to a boil, lower heat, and simmer 30 minutes.

Strain through a fine sieve, discarding vegetables, etc. Clean saucepan and return soup to saucepan. Bring to a boil. Whisk in crème fraiche and thicken with cornstarch mixture. Season with crayfish liquid, salt and pepper.

Season with cognac or Madeira and whisk in butter with an immersion blender just before serving.

Pie:
Preheat oven to 175° C (350° F).

Crumble butter into flour until consistency of large crumbs. Quickly mix in water to form a light pastry. Do not overwork. Or combine in a food processor. Add water and process only until pastry cleans sides.

Roll out and press pastry into eight individual pie pans or one large. Line pie shells with parchment paper and fill with dried peas, beans or rice. Freeze 10 minutes. Bake about 10 minutes, then remove paper and peas.

Lower heat to 150°C (300°F). Pour in pie filling and bake until set, about 15 minutes for individual pies, 30 minutes for one large.

Place crayfish tails in soup bowls and fill with hot soup. Serve with lukewarm pies.

Saffron rolls

Saffransbullar

ABOUT 30 ROLLS

175 G (6 OZ) UNSALTED BUTTER
5 DL (2 CUPS) MILK
50 G (1 3/4 OZ) FRESH YEAST
1/2 TEASPOON SALT
1 3/4 DL (3/4 CUP) SUGAR
1 G (1/2 TS) GROUND SAFFRON
1 EGG (OPTIONAL)
1–1 1/2 DL (1/2–2/3 CUP) RAISINS
ABOUT 1 1/2 LITERS (6 1/2 CUPS)
ALL-PURPOSE FLOUR
1 EGG

Melt butter, add milk and heat to 37°C
(98°F). Crumble yeast into some of milk
mixture and stir until dissolved. Add
remaining liquid, salt, sugar, saffron,
egg (if desired) and raisins. Knead in,
by machine or by hand, enough flour
to make a smooth and elastic dough
that cleans bowl. Sprinkle with flour,
cover and let rise in a warm place
about 30 minutes.

Knead dough in bowl a few minutes,
then turn onto floured board and knead
until smooth.

Form into rolls and garnish with raisins.
Place on greased baking sheets. Cover
and let rise in a warm place until almost
doubled, about 30 minutes.

Preheat oven to 225°C (425°F). Lightly
beat egg and brush on rolls. Bake 5–10
minutes. Cool covered.

The celebration of St. Lucia's Day, December
13, is a unique ritual in Sweden. Throughout
the country, girls don candle crowns and serve
saffron rolls, called *lussekatter*, or "Lucy's
cats", to their family.

Gingerbread cookies

Pepparkakor

ABOUT 150 COOKIES

3 DL (1 1/4 CUPS) SUGAR
1/2 DL (3 1/2 TABLESPOONS) DARK CORN
SYRUP
1 DL (SCANT 1/2 CUP) WATER
200 G (7 OZ) UNSALTED BUTTER
1 TABLESPOON GROUND BITTER
ORANGE PEEL
1–2 TABLESPOONS GROUND CINNAMON
1/2 TABLESPOON GROUND GINGER
1/2 TABLESPOON GROUND CLOVES
2 TEASPOONS GROUND CARDAMOM
2 TEASPOONS BAKING SODA
ABOUT 1 LITER (4 1/4 CUPS) ALL-PURPOSE
FLOUR
WHOLE OR HALVED ALMONDS (OPTIONAL)

Bring sugar, syrup and water to a boil.
Place butter and spices in a large bowl.
Pour over hot sugar mixture. Stir until
butter is melted. Cool.

Combine baking soda with most of the
flour and add. Knead lightly to form a
smooth dough. Do not overwork. Wrap
in plastic and refrigerate overnight.

Preheat oven to 200°C (400°F). Roll
a small amount of dough at a time on
a floured board with light strokes. Cut
out figures with cookie cutters. Garnish
cookies with almonds, if desired.

Place cookies on cold, greased baking
sheets or on baking parchment. Cook on
center oven shelf 5–8 minutes. Keep a
watchful eye. These cookies burn easily.

Gingerbread cookies are true comfort food
during long, dark Swedish winters. They
are served from the first Sunday in Advent
through Christmas.

Beef Rydberg with mustard cream

Biff Rydberg med senapsgrädde

4 SERVINGS

500 G (1 1/4 LB) BEEF TENDERLOIN
8 MEDIUM POTATOES
2 ONIONS
BUTTER
SALT AND PEPPER
1 TABLESPOON CHOPPED PARSLEY
WORCESTERSHIRE SAUCE

Cut meat into 1 cm (1/2") cubes.
Peel potatoes and cut into 1 1/2 cm
(3/4") cubes. Mince onions.

Fry potatoes slowly in butter until
lightly browned, but soft inside.

Sweat onions in butter until soft and
transparent. Salt and pepper meat.
Fry quickly over high heat, so meat
is browned yet pink inside.

Arrange on a platter with potatoes on
one side, meat on the other, onions in
between. Sprinkle with chopped parsley
and a few drops Worcestershire sauce.
Serve with mustard cream.

Mustard cream:
4 SERVINGS

2 TEASPOONS DRY MUSTARD
2 TEASPOONS SUGAR
1 DL (SCANT 1/2 CUP) WHIPPING CREAM

Combine mustard and sugar and whisk
into cream. Whip until stiff.

Years ago, the elegant Hotel Rydberg was the
pride of Gustav Adolf Square in Stockholm.
Its restaurant was the favorite haunt of actors
and artists. This dish probably originated there.

Lenten buns

Semlor

10–12 BUNS

Buns:
75 G (2 3/4 OZ) BUTTER
3 DL (1 1/4 CUPS) MILK
50 G (1 3/4 OZ) FRESH YEAST
1/2 TEASPOON SALT
1 DL (1/2 CUP) SUGAR
1 EGG
1/2 TEASPOON HORNSALT (OR
1 1/2 TEASPOONS BAKING POWDER)
ABOUT 9 DL (3 3/4 CUPS) ALL-PURPOSE
FLOUR
1 EGG

Filling:
100 G (4 OZ, 3/4 CUP) ALMONDS
CRUMBS FROM INSIDE ROLLS
1 DL (1/2 CUP) SUGAR
ABOUT 1 DL (1/2 CUP) MILK OR CREAM

Garnish:
2 DL (3/4 CUP) WHIPPING CREAM
1 TABLESPOON CONFECTIONER'S SUGAR

Melt butter, add milk and heat to 37°C (98°F). Crumble yeast into some of milk mixture and stir until dissolved. Add remaining liquid, salt, sugar and egg. Combine hornsalt with some of the flour. Knead in enough flour to make a smooth and elastic dough that cleans bowl. Cover and let rise in a warm place until almost doubled, 20–30 minutes.

Turn dough onto floured board and knead in remaining flour. Form into 10–12 smooth, round rolls. Place on greased baking sheet. Cover and let rise in a warm place about 20 minutes.

Preheat oven to 250°C (475°F). Lightly beat egg and brush on rolls. Bake 5–10 minutes. Transfer to a rack. Cool covered.

Blanch, peel and grind almonds. Cut top off each roll. Remove most of center, but do not go through crust. Combine center crumbs with almonds, sugar and milk or cream. Filling should be quite loose. Divide filling among rolls.

Whip cream and divide among rolls. Return tops and sprinkle with confectioner's sugar.

Filled buns should be eaten the day they are made. Plain buns can be frozen 3–6 months.

It is possible to use purchased almond paste in the filling. Count on 100–150 g (3 1/2–5 oz) almond paste for one batch of buns. Grate almond paste and combine with crumbs and milk or cream.

These buns are meant to be eaten during Lent, but now everyone in Sweden enjoys these delicious treats from January through Easter.

Waffles with raspberry jam

Våfflor med hallonsylt

ABOUT 12 WAFFLES

4 DL (1 2/3 CUPS) WHIPPING CREAM
4 DL (1 2/3 CUPS) ALL-PURPOSE FLOUR
3 DL (1 1/4 CUPS) ICE WATER OR ICE COLD
SODA WATER
100 G (3 1/2 OZ) MELTED UNSALTED
BUTTER (LUKEWARM)

Combine all ingredients and mix until smooth.

Cook in a waffle iron. When done, place on a rack. Just before serving, stack.

Serve with raspberry or cloudberry jam and whipped cream.

Raspberry jam:
ABOUT 2 1/2 LITERS (QUARTS)

4 LITERS (16 2/3 CUPS) RASPBERRIES
1 1/4 LITERS (5 CUPS) SUGAR
SCANT 1/2 TEASPOON SODIUM BENZOATE
SCANT 1/2 TEASPOON POTASSIUM SORBATE

Clean berries. Layer berries and sugar in a large pot. Let steep a few hours. Slowly heat to boiling, then simmer slowly 15–20 minutes. Shake and turn pot so mixture cooks evenly. Skim well.

The jam is ready when berries fill with liquid and sink to bottom.

Dissolve preservatives in a little berry liquid and stir into mixture.

Pour into hot, clean jars. Screw lid on tightly while jam is still hot.

This recipe can be used with strawberries or blueberries or any mixture of the above.

Waffles are a delicious, thoroughly useless delicacy, enjoyed year-round throughout Sweden. Whipped cream and jam are the best accompaniments.

Recipe index

A journey through Sweden

This book is the result of a journey all over Sweden. During all four seasons, we have traveled around and tasted the best this country has to offer. From Lappland in the far north, where the Sami live with their flocks of reindeer, to Skåne in the south, with its broad plains.

During the winter, we saw the snow fall over the mountains in Åre. In the spring we saw the Tännfors rapids swirl through Jämtland. In the summer, we visited glass artist Ulrika Hydman-Vallien right in the center of Småland's glass country. And in the fall, we took part in the apple harvest in Skåne and lobster fishing in Bohuslän, until the force of the wind reminded us that another winter was approaching.

A year in Sweden. A journey through ever-changing nature. A journey which has led to this recipe collection, which we hope will sum up the versatile, colorful and wonderful Swedish kitchen.

Our warm thanks to all the fantastic people who helped Ingela and Milis during the journey through Sweden.

Bengt and Britt-Marie Peterson, Käringön
Göran and Annika Grundén, Käringön
Anders Björklund, Åre
Ulrika Hydman-Vallien, Åfors
Klas-Göran and
Elisabeth Önnhall, Lycksele
Ulla Alvarsson, Malå
Sanfred and Börje Stenlund
Renen Kalle
Gun Olsson, Nusnäs
Marianne Malmström
Jan Jonsson, Kivik
Danderyd's folk dance troop
Vetekatten

PROJECT LEADER: Ingela Holm
RECIPES: Malin Söderström
TEXT: Jan Gradvall
PHOTOGRAPHERS: Wolfgang Kleinschmidt, food and Marie-Louise Nilsson, on location.
GRAPHIC DESIGN: Pelle Holm and Kjell Benettsson
ENGLISH TRANSLATION AND RECIPE ADAPTATION: Melody Favish

Printed by Abildgaard Grafisk, Denmark 2005

Forma Publishing Group is milieucertified according to ISO 14001

First edition, fifth printing 2005

© 2000 authors and ICA bokförlag, Forma Publishing Group AB, Västerås

www.formapg.se/bok

ISBN 91-534-2119-1